I0163110

The Silk-Hat Soldier & Other Poems in War Time by Richard le Gallienne

Richard Thomas Gallienne was born in Liverpool on 20th January, 1866.

His first job was in an accountant's office, but this was quickly abandoned to pursue his first love as a professional writer. His first work, My Ladies' Sonnets, was published in 1887.

In 1889 he became, for a brief time, literary secretary to Wilson Barrett the manager, actor, and playwright. Barrett enjoyed immense success with the staging of melodramas, which would later reach a peak with the historical tragedy The Sign of the Cross (1895).

Le Gallienne joined the staff of The Star newspaper in 1891, and also wrote for various other papers under the pseudonym 'Logroller'. He contributed to the short-lived but influential quarterly periodical The Yellow Book, published between 1894 and 1897.

His first wife, Mildred Lee, died in 1894 leaving their daughter, Hesper, in his care.

In 1897 he married the Danish journalist Julie Norregard. However, the marriage would not be a success. She left him in 1903 and took their daughter Eva to live in Paris. They were eventually divorced in June 1911.

Le Gallienne now moved to the United States and became resident there.

On 27th October 1911, he married Mrs. Irma Perry, whose marriage to her first cousin, the painter and sculptor Roland Hinton Perry, had been dissolved in 1904. Le Gallienne and Irma had known each other for many years and had written an article together a few years earlier in 1906.

Le Gallienne and Irma lived in Paris from the late 1920s, where Irma's daughter Gwen was by then an established figure in the expatriate bohème. Le Gallienne also added a regular newspaper column to the frequent publication of his poems, essays and other articles.

By 1930 Le Gallienne's book publishing career had virtually ceased. During the latter years of that decade Le Gallienne lived in Menton on the French Riviera and, during the war years, in nearby Monaco. His house was commandeered by German troops and his handsome library was nearly sent back to Germany as bounty. Le Gallienne managed a successful appeal to a German officer in Monaco which allowed him to return to Menton to collect his books.

To his credit Le Gallienne refused to write propaganda for the local German and Italian authorities, and financially was often in dire need. On one occasion he collapsed in the street due to hunger.

Richard Thomas Gallienne died on 15th September 1947. He is buried in Menton in a grave whose lease is, at present, due to expire in 2023.

Index of Contents

To Belgium

Our tears, our songs, our laurels—what are these
To thee in thy Gethsemane of loss,
Stretched in thine unimagined agonies
On Hell's last engine of the Iron Cross.

For such a world as this that thou shouldst die
Is price too vast—yet, Belgium, hadst thou sold

Thyself, O then had fled from out the earth
Honour for ever, and left only Gold.

Nor diest thou—for soon shalt thou awake,
And, lifted high on our victorious shields,
Watch the new sunrise driving for your sons
The hated German shadow from your fields.

"British colonists resident in London volunteer, and not even silk hats are doffed before training begins"
—New York Times

The Silk-Hat Soldier

I saw him in a picture, and I felt I'd like to cry—
He stood in line,
The man "for mine,"
A tall silk-hatted "guy"—
Right on the call,
Silk hat and all,
He'd hurried to the cry—
For he loves England well enough for England to die.

I've seen King Harry's helmet in the Abbey hanging high—
The one he wore
At Agincourt;
But braver to my eye
That city toff
Too keen to doff
His stove-pipe—bless him—why?
For he loves England well enough for England to die.

And other fellows in that line had come too on the fly,
Their joys and toys,
Brave English boys,
For good and all put by;
O you brave best,
Teach all the rest
How pure the heart and high
When one loves England well enough for England to die.

One threw his cricket-bat aside, one left the ink to dry;
All peace and play
He's put away,
And bid his love good-bye—
O mother mine!
O sweetheart mine!

No man of yours am I—
If I love not England well enough for England to die.

I guess it strikes a chill somewhere, the bravest won't deny,
All that you love,
Away to shove,
And set your teeth to die;
But better dead,
When all is said,
Than lapped in peace to lie—
If we love not England well enough for England to die.

The Cry of the Little Peoples

The Cry of the Little Peoples went up to God in vain;
The Czech and the Pole, and the Finn, and the Schleswig Dane:

We ask but a little portion of the green, ambitious earth;
Only to sow and sing and reap in the land of our birth.

We ask not coaling stations, nor ports in the China seas,
We leave to the big child-nations such rivalries as these.

We have learned the lesson of Time, and we know three things of worth;
Only to sow and sing and reap in the land of our birth.

O leave us little margins, waste ends of land and sea,
A little grass, and a hill or two, and a shadowing tree;

O leave us our little rivers that sweetly catch the sky,
To drive our mills, and to carry our wood, and to ripple by.

Once long ago, as you, with hollow pursuit of fame,
We filled all the shaking world with the sound of our name,

But now are we glad to rest, our battles and boasting done,
Glad just to sow and sing and reap in our share of the sun.

Of this O will ye rob us,—with a foolish mighty hand,
Add with such cruel sorrow, so small a land to your land?

So might a boy rejoice him to conquer a hive of bees,
Overcome ants in battle,—we are scarcely more mighty than these—

So might a cruel heart hear a nightingale singing alone,
And say, "I am mighty! See how the singing stops with a stone!"

Yea, he were mighty indeed, mighty to crush and to gain;
But the bee and the ant and the bird were the mighty of brain.

And what shall you gain if you take us and bind us and beat us with thongs,
And drive us to sing underground in a whisper our sad little songs?

Forbid us the very use of our heart's own nursery tongue—
Is this to be strong, ye nations, is this to be strong?

Your vulgar battles to fight, and your grocery conquests to keep,
For this shall we break our hearts, for this shall our old men weep?

What gain in the day of battle—to the Russ, to the German, what gain,
The Czech, and the Pole, and the Finn, and the Schleswig Dane?

The Cry of the Little Peoples goes up to God in vain,
For the world is given over to the cruel sons of Cain;

The hand that would bless us is weak, and the hand that would break us is strong,
And the power of pity is nought but the power of a song.

The dreams that our fathers dreamed to-day are laughter and dust,
And nothing at all in the world is left for a man to trust;

Let us hope no more, or dream, or prophesy, or pray,
For the iron world no less will crash on its iron way;

Yea! nothing is left but to watch, with a helpless, pitying eye,
The kind old aims for the world, and the kind old fashions die.

The Illusion of War

War
I abhor,
And yet how sweet
The sound along the marching street
Of drum and fife, and I forget
Wet eyes of widows, and forget
Broken old mothers, and the whole
Dark butchery without a soul.

Without a soul—save this bright drink
Of heady music, sweet as hell;
And even my peace-abiding feet
Go marching with the marching street,

For yonder, yonder goes the fife,
And what care I for human life!
The tears fill my astonished eyes
And my full heart is like to break,
And yet 'tis all embannered lies,
A dream those little drummers make.

O it is wickedness to clothe
Yon hideous grinning thing that stalks
Hidden in music, like a queen
That in a garden of glory walks,
Till good men love the thing they loathe.
Art, thou hast many infamies,
But not an infamy like this;
O snap the fife and still the drum,
And show the monster as she is.

Christmas in War-Time

I

This is the year that has no Christmas Day,
Even the little children must be told
That something sad is happening far away—
Or, if you needs must play,
As children must,
Play softly children, underneath your breath!
For over our hearts hangs low the shadow of death,
Those hearts to you mysteriously old,
Grim grown-up hearts that ponder night and day
On the straight lists of broken-hearted dead,
Black narrow lists no tears can wash away,
Reading in which one cries out here and here
And falls into a dream upon a name.
Be happy softly, children, for a woe
Is on us, a great woe for little fame,—
Ah! in the old woods leave the mistletoe,
And leave the holly for another year,
Its berries are too red.

II

And lovers, like to children, will not you
Cease for a little from your kissing mirth,
Thinking of other lovers that must go

Kissed back with fire into the bosom of earth,
Ah! in the old woods leave the mistletoe,
Be happy, softly, lovers, for you too
Shall be as sad as they another year,
And then for you the holly be berries of blood,
And mistletoe strange berries of bitter tears.
Ah! lovers, leave you your beatitude,
Give your sad eyes and ears
To the far griefs of neighbour and of friend,
To the great loves that find a little end,
Long loves that in a sudden puff of fire
With a wild thought expire.

III

And you, ye merchants, you that eat and cheat,
Gold-seeking hucksters in a noble land,
Think, when you lift the wine up in your hand,
Of a fierce vintage tragically red,
Red wine of the hearts of English soldiers dead,
Who ran to a wild death with laughing feet—
That we may sleep and drink and eat and cheat.
Ah! you brave few that fight for all the rest,
And die with smiling faces strangely blest,
Because you die for England—O to do
Something again for you,
In this great deed to have some little part;
To send so great a message from the heart
Of England that one man shall be as ten,
Hearing how England loves her Englishmen!
Ah! think you that a single gun is fired
We do not hear in England. Ah! we hear,
And mothers go with proud unhappy eyes
That say: It is for England that he dies,
England that does the cruel work of God,
And gives her well beloved to save the world.
For this is death like to a woman desired,
For this the wine-press trod.

IV

And you in churches, praying this Christmas morn,
Pray as you never prayed that this may be
The little war that brought the great world peace;
Undazzled with its glorious infamy,
O pray with all your hearts that war may cease,

And who knows but that God may hear the prayer.
So it may come about next Christmas Day
That we shall hear the happy children play
Gladly aloud, unmindful of the dead,
And watch the lovers go
To the old woods to find the mistletoe.
But this year, children, if you needs must play,
Play very softly, underneath your breath;
Be happy softly, lovers, for great Death
Makes England holy with sorrow this Christmas Day;
Yes! in the old woods leave the mistletoe,
And leave the holly for another year—
Its berries are too red.

Christmas, 1899—Written during the Boer War.

"Soldier Going to the War"

Soldier going to the war—
Will you take my heart with you,
So that I may share a little
In the famous things you do?

Soldier going to the war—
If in battle you must fall,
Will you, among all the faces,
See my face the last of all?

Soldier coming from the war—
Who shall bind your sunburnt brow
With the laurel of the hero,
Soldier, soldier—vow for vow!

Soldier coming from the war—
When the street is one wide sea,
Flags and streaming eyes and glory—
Soldier, will you look for me?

The Rainbow

"These things are real," said one, and bade me gaze
On black and mighty shapes of iron and stone,
On murder, on madness, on lust, on towns ablaze,
And on a thing made all of rattling bone:

"What," said he, "will you bring to match with these?"
"Yea! War is real," I said, "and real is Death,
A little while—mortal realities;
But Love and Hope draw an immortal breath."

Think you the storm that wrecks a summer day,
With funeral blackness and with leaping fire
And boiling roar of rain, more real than they
That, when the warring heavens begin to tire,
With tender fingers on the tumult paint;
Spanning the huddled wrack from base to cope
With soft effulgence, like some haloed saint,—
The rainbow bridge eternal that is Hope.

Deem her no phantom born of desperate dreams:
Ere man yet was, 'twas hope that wrought him man;
The blind earth, climbing skyward by her gleams,
Hoped—and the beauty of the world began.
Prophetic of all loveliness to be,
Though God Himself seem from His station hurled,
Still shall the blackest hell look up and see
Hope's rainbow on the summits of the world.

A Lost Hour

God gave us an hour for our tears,
One hour out of all the years,
For all the years were another's gold,
Given in a cruel troth of old.

And how did we spend his boon?
That sweet miraculous flower
Born to die in an hour,
Late born to die so soon.

Did we watch it with breathless breath
By slow degrees unfold?
Did we taste the innermost heart of it
The honey of each sweet part of it?
Suck all its hidden gold
To the very dregs of its death?

Nay, this is all we did with our hour-
We tore it to pieces, that precious flower;
Like any daisy, with listless mirth,
We shed its petals upon the earth;

And, children-like, when it all was done,
We cried unto God for another one.

All the Words in All the World

All the flowers cannot weave
A garland worthy of your hair,
Not a bird in the four winds
Can sing of you that is so fair.

Only the spheres can sing of you;
Some planet in celestial space,
Hallowed and lonely in the dawn,
Shall sing the poem of your face.

The Afternoon Is Lonely For Your Face

The afternoon is lonely for your face,
The pampered morning mocks the day's decline
I was so rich at noon, the sun was mine,
Mine the sad sea that in that rocky place
Girded us round with blue betrothal ring.
Because your heart was mine, your heart, that precious thing.

The night will be a desert till the dawn,
Unless you take some ferry-boat of dreams,
And glide to me, a glory of silver beams,
Under my eyelids, like sad curtains drawn;
So, by good hap, my heart can find its way
Where all your sweetness lies in fragrant disarray.

Ah! but with morn the world begins anew,
Again the sea shall sing up to your feet,
And earth and all the heavens call you sweet,
You all alone with me, I all alone with you,
And all the business of the laurelled hours
Shyly to gaze on that betrothal ring of ours.

After The War

After the war—I hear men ask—what then?
As tho this rock-ribbed world, sculptured with fire,

And bastioned deep in the ethereal plan,
Can never be its morning self again
Because of this brief madness, man with man;

How many wars and long-forgotten woes
Unnumbered, nameless, made a like despair
In hearts long stilled; how many suns have set
On burning cities blackening the air,—
Yet dawn came dreaming back, her lashes wet
With dew, and daisies in her innocent hair.

Nor shall, for this, the soul's ascension pause,
Nor the sure evolution of the laws
That out of foulness lift the flower to sun,
And out of fury forge the evening star.

Deem not Love's building of the world undone—
Far Love's beginning was, her end is far;
By paths of fire and blood her feet must climb,
Seeking a loveliness she scarcely knows,
Whose meaning is beyond the reach of Time.

Ballade of the Absent Guest

Friends whom to-night once more I greet,
Most glad am I with you to be,
And, as I look around, I meet
Many a face right good to see;
But one I miss—ah! where is he?—
Of merry eye and sparkling jest,
Who used to brim my glass for me;
I drink—in what?—the Absent Guest.

Low lies he in his winding-sheet,
By organized hypocrisy
Hurled from his happy wine-clad seat,
Stilled his kind heart and hushed his glee;
His very name daren't mention we,
That good old friend who brought such zest,
And set our tongues and spirits free:
I drink—in what?—the Absent Guest.

No choice to-night 'twixt 'dry' or 'sweet,'
'Twixt red or white, 'twixt Rye,—ah! me—
Or Scotch—and think! we live to see't—
No whispered word, nor massive fee,

Nor even influenza plea,
Can raise a bubble; but, as best
We may, we make our hollow spree:
I drink—in what?—the Absent Guest.

ENVOI

Friends, good is coffee, good is tea,
And water has a charm unguessed—
And yet—that brave old deity!
I drink—in tears—the Absent Guest.

Ballade of the Dead Face That Never Dies

The peril of fair faces all his days
No man shall 'scape: be it for joy or woe,
Each is the thrall of some predestined face
Divinely doomed to work his overthrow,
Transiently fair, as flowers in gardens blow,
Then fade, and charm no more our listless eyes;
But some fair faces ever fairer grow—
Beware of the dead face that never dies.

No snare young beauty for thy manhood lays,
No honeyed kiss the girls of Paphos know,
Shall hold thee as the silent smiling ways
Of her that went—yet only seemed to go—
With April blossoms and with last year's snow;
Each year she comes again in subtler guise,
And beckons us to her green bed below—
Beware of the dead face that never dies.

The living fade before her lunar gaze,
Her phantom youth their ruddy veins out-glow,
She lays cold fingers on the lips that praise
Aught save her lovely face of long ago;
Oblivious poppies all in vain we sow
Before the opening gates of Paradise;
There shalt thou find her pacing to and fro—
Beware of the dead face that never dies.

ENVOI

Prince, take thy fill of love, for even so
Sad men grow happy and no other wise;
But love the quick—and as thy mortal foe

Beware of the dead face that never dies.

Ballade To A Departing God

God of the Wine List, roseate lord,
And is it really then good-by?
Of Prohibitionists abhorred,
Must thou in sorry sooth then die,
(O fatal morning of July!)
Nor aught hold back the threatened hour
That shrinks thy purple clusters dry?
Say not good-by—but _au revoir_!

For the last time the wine is poured,
For the last toast the glass raised high,
And henceforth round the wintry board,
As dumb as fish, we'll sit and sigh,
And eat our Puritanic pie,
And dream of suppers gone before,
With flying wit and words that fly—
Say not good-by—but _au revoir_!

'Twas on thy wings the poet soared,
And Sorrow fled when thou wentst by,
And, when we said 'Here's looking toward' . . .
It seemed a better world, say I,
With greener grass and bluer sky . . .
The writ is on the Tavern Door,
And who would tipple on the sly? . . .
'Tis not good-by—but _au revoir_!

ENVOI

Gay God of Bottles, I deny
Those brave tempestuous times are o'er;
Somehow I think, I scarce know why,
'Tis not good-by—but au revoir!

Ballade of the Paid Puritan

In vain with whip and knotted cord
The hirelings of hypocrisy
Would make us comely for the Lord:
Think ye God works through such as ye—

Paid Puritan, plump Pharisee,
And lobbyist fingering his fat bill,
Reeking of rum and bribery:
God needs not you to work His will.

We know you whom you serve, abhorred
Traducers of true piety,
What tarnished gold is your reward
In Washington and Albany;
'Tis not from God you take your fee,
Another's purpose to fulfil,
You that are God's worst enemy:
God needs not you to work His will.

Not by the money-changing horde,
Base traders in the sanctuary,
Nor by fanatic fire and sword,
Shall man grow as God wills him be;
In his own heart a voice hath he
That whispers to him small and still;
God gives him eyes His good to see:
God needs not you to work His will.

ENVOI

Dear Prince, a sinner's honesty
Is more to God, much nearer still,
Than the bribed hypocritic knee:
God needs not you to work His will.

Beauty's Wardrobe

My love said she had nought to wear;
Her garments all were old,
And soon her body must go bare
Against the winter's cold.

I took her out into the dawn,
And from the mountain's crest
Unwound long wreaths of misty lawn,
And wound them round her breast.

Then passed we to the maple grove,
Like a great hall of gold,
The yellow and the red we wove
In rustling flounce and fold.

'Now, love,' said I, 'go, do it on!
And I would have you note
No lovely lady dead and gone
Had such a petticoat.'

Then span I out of milkweeds fine
Fair stockings soft and long,
And other things of quaint design
That unto maids belong.

And beads of amber and of pearl
About her neck I strung,
And in the bronze of her thick hair
The purple grape I hung. . . .

Then led her to a glassy spring,
And bade her look and see
If any girl in all the world
Had such fine clothes as she.

Blue Flower

Blue flower waving in the wind,
Say whose blue eyes
Lift up your swaying fragile stem
To the blue skies.

Is she a queen that lies asleep
In a green hill,
With all her silver ornaments
Around her still?

Or is she but a simple girl,
Whose boy was drowned,
In some cold sea, some stormy morn,
On some blue sound?

Immortality

"This hot, hard flame with which our bodies burn
Will make some meadow blaze with daffodil;
Ay! and those argent breasts of thine will turn
To water-lilies; the brown fields men till

Will be more fruitful for our love to-night:
Nothing is lost in Nature; all things live in Death's despite.

"So when men bury us beneath the yew
Thy crimson-stained mouth a rose will be,
And thy soft eyes lush blue-bells dimmed with dew;
And when the white narcissus wantonly
Kisses the wind, its playmate, some faint joy
Will thrill our dust, and we will be again fond maid and boy.

"… How my heart leaps up
To think of that grand living after death
In beast and bird and flower, when this cup,
Being filled too full of spirit, bursts for breath,
And with the pale leaves of some autumn day,
The soul, earth's earliest conqueror, becomes earth's last great prey.

"O think of it! We shall inform ourselves
Into all sensuous life; the goat-foot faun,
The centaur, or the merry, bright-eyed elves
That leave they: dancing rings to spite the dawn
Upon the meadows, shall not be more near
Than you and I to Nature's mysteries, for we shall hear

"The thrush's heart beat, and the daisies grow,
And the wan snowdrop sighing for the sun
On sunless days in winter; we shall know
By whom the silver gossamer is spun,
Who paints the diapered fritillaries,
On what wide wings from shivering pine to pine the eagle flies.

"We shall be notes in that great symphony
Whose cadence circles through the rhythmic spheres,
And all the live world's throbbing heart shall be
One with our heart; the stealthy, creeping years
Have lost their terrors now; we shall not die—
The universe itself shall be our Immortality!'

In The City

Away from the silent hills and the talking of upland waters,
The high still stars and the lonely moon in her quarters,
I fly to the city, the streets, the faces, the towers;
And I leave behind me the hush and the dews and the flowers,
The mink that steals by the stream a-shimmer among the rocks,
The hawk o'er the barn-yard sailing, the little cub-bear and the fox,

The woodchuck and his burrow, and the little snake at noon,
And the house of the yellow-jacket, and the cricket's endless tune.

And what shall I find in the city that shall take the place of these?
O I shall find my love there, and fall at her silken knees,
And for the moon her breast, and for the stars her eyes,
And under her shadowed hair the gardens of Paradise.

In The Night

'Kiss me, dear Love!'
But there was none to hear,
Only the darkness round about my bed
And hollow silence, for thy face had fled,
Though in my dreaming it had come so near.

I slept again and it came back to me,
Burning within the hollow arch of night
Like some fair flame of sacrificial light,
And all my soul sprang up to mix with thee-
'Kiss me, my love!
Ah, Love, thy face how fair!'
So did I cry, but still thou wert not there.

Love Eternal

The human heart will never change,
The human dream will still go on,
The enchanted earth be ever strange
With moonlight and the morning sun,
And still the seas shall shout for joy,
And swing the stars as in a glass,
The girl be angel for the boy,
The lad be hero for the lass.

The fashions of our mortal brains
New names for dead men's thoughts shall give,
But we find not for all our pains
Why 'tis so wonderful to live;
The beauty of a meadow-flower
Shall make a mock of all our skill,
And God, upon his lonely tower
Shall keep his secret—secret still.

The old magician of the skies,
With coloured and sweet-smelling things,
Shall charm the sense and trance the eyes,
Still onward through a million springs;
And nothing old and nothing new
Into the magic world be born,
Yea! nothing older than the dew,
And nothing younger than the morn.

Delight and Destiny and Death
Shall still the mortal story weave,
Man shall not lengthen out his breath,
Nor stay when it is time to leave;
And all in vain for him to ask
His little meaning in the Whole,
Done well or ill his tiny task,
The mystic making of his soul.

Ah! love, and is it not enough
To have our part in this romance
Made of such planetary stuff,
Strange partners in the cosmic dance?
Though Life be all too swift a dream,
And its fair rose must fade and fall,
Life has no sorrow in its scheme
As never to have lived at all.

This fire that through our being runs,
When our two hearts together beat,
Is one with yonder burning sun's,
Two atoms that in glory meet;
What unimagined loss it were,
If that dread power in which we trust
Had left your eyes, your lips, your hair,
Nought but un-animated dust.

Unknown the thrilling touch divine
That sets our magic clay aflame,
That wrought your beauty to be mine,
And joy enough to speak your name;
Thanks be to Life that did this thing,
Unsought, beloved, for you and me,
Gave us the rose, and birds to sing,
The golden earth, the blue-robed sea.

Love Platonic

Surely at last, O Lady, the sweet moon
That bringeth in the happy singing weather
Groweth to pearly queendom, and full soon
Shall Love and Song go hand in hand together;
For all the pain that all too long hath waited
In deep dumb darkness shall have speech at last,
And the bright babe Death gave the Love he mated
Shall leap to light and kiss the weeping past.

For all the silver morning is a-glimmer
With gleaming spears of great Apollo's host,
And the night fadeth like a spent out swimmer
Hurled from the headlands of some shining coast.
O, happy soul, thy mouth at last is singing,
Drunken with wine of morning's azure deep,
Sing on, my soul, the world beneath thee swinging,
A bough of song above a sea of sleep.

Who is the lady I sing?
Ah, how can I tell thee her praise
For whom all my life's but the string
Of a rosary painful of days;

Which I count with a curious smile
As a miser who hoardeth his gain,
Though, a madhearted spendthrift the while,
I but gather to waste again.

Yea, I pluck from the tree of the years,
As a country maid greedy of flowers,
Each day brimming over with tears,
And I scatter like petals its hours;

And I trample them under my feet
In a frenzy of cloven-hoofed swine,
And the breath of their dying is sweet,
And the blood of their hearts is as wine.

O, I throw me low down on the ground
And I bury my face in their death,
And only I rise at the sound
Of a wind as it scattereth,

As it scattereth sweetly the dried
Leaves withered and brittle and sere

Of days of old years that have died-
And, O, it is sweet in my ear

And I rise me and build me a pyre
Of the whispering skeleton things,
And my heart laugheth low with the fire,
Laugheth high with the flame as it springs;

And above in the flickering glare
I mark me the boughs of my tree,
My tree of the years, growing bare.
Growing bare with the scant days to be.

Then I turn to my beads and I pray
For the axe at the root of the tree-
Last flower, last bead-ah! last day
That shall part me, my darling, from thee!

And I pray for the knife on the string
Of this rosary painful of days:
But who is the Lady I sing?
Ah, how can I tell thee her praise!

II

I make this rhyme of my lady and me
To give me ease of my misery,
Of my lady and me I make this rhyme
For lovers in the after-time.
And I weave its warp from day to day
In a golden loom deep hid away
In my secret heart, where no one goes
But my lady's self, and-no one knows.

With bended head all day I pore
On a joyless task, and yet before
My eyes all day, through each weary hour,
Breathes my lady's face like a dewy flower.
Like rain it comes through the dusty air,
Like sun on the meadows to think of her;
O sweet as violets in early spring
The flower-girls to the city bring,
O, healing-bright to wintry eyes
As primrose-gold 'neath northern skies-
But O for fit thing to compare
With the joy I have in the thought of her!
So all day long doth her holy face

Bring fragrance to the barren place,
And whensoe'er it comes nearest me,
My loom it weaveth busily.

Some days there be when the loom is still
And my soul is sad as an autumn hill,
But how to tell the blessed time
When my heart is one glowing prayer of rhyme!
Think on the humming afternoon
Within some busy wood in June,
When nettle patches, drunk with the sun,
Are fiery outposts of the shade;
While gnats keep up a dizzy reel,
And the grasshopper, perched upon his blade,
Loud drones his fairy threshing-wheel:-
Hour when some poet-wit might feign
The drowsy tune of the throbbing air
The weaving of the gossamer
In secret nooks of wood and lane-
The gossamer, silk night-robes of the flowers,
Fluttered apart by amorous morning hours.
Yea, as the weaving of the gossamer,
If truly that the mystic golden boom,
Is the strange rapture of my hidden loom,
As I sit in the light of the thought of her;
And it weaveth, weaveth, day by day,
This parti-coloured roundelay;
Weaving for ease of misery,
Weaving this rhyme of my lady and me,
Weaving, weaving this warp of rhyme
For lovers in the after-time.

My lady, lover, may never be mine
In the same sweet way that thine is thine,
My lady and I may never stand
By the holy altar hand in hand,
My lady and I may never rest
Through the golden midnight breast to breast,
Nor share long days of happy light
Sweet moving in each other's sight:
Yea, even must we ever miss
The honey of the chastest kiss.

III

But, Song, arise thee on a greater wing,
Nor twitter robin-like of love, nor sing

A pretty dalliance with grief-but try
Some metre like a sky,
Wherein to set
Stars that may linger yet
When I, thy master, shall have come to die.
Twitter and tweet
Thy carollings
Of little things,
Of fair and sweet;
For it is meet,
O robin red!
That little theme
Hath little song,
That little head
Hath little dream,
And long.
But we have starry business, such a grief
As Autumn's, dead by some forgotten sheaf,
While all the distance echoes of the wain;
Grief as an ocean's for some sudden isle
Of living green that stayed with it a while,
Then to oblivious deluge plunged again!
Grief as of Alps that yearn but never reach,
Grief as of Death for Life, of Night for Day:
Such grief, O Song, how hast thou strength to teach,
How hope to make assay?

Love's Arithmetic

You often ask me, love, how much I love you,
Bidding my fancy find
An answer to your mind;
I say: 'Past count, as there are stars above you.'
You shake your head and say,
'Many and bright are they,
But that is not enough.'

Again I try:
'If all the leaves on all the trees
Were counted over,
And all the waves on all the seas,
More times your lover,
Yea! more than twice ten thousand times am I.'
''Tis not enough,' again you make reply.

'How many blades of grass,' one day I said,

'Are there from here to China? how many bees
Have gathered honey through the centuries?
Tell me how many roses have bloomed red
Since the first rose till this rose in your hair?
How many butterflies are born each year?
How many raindrops are there in a shower?
How many kisses, darling, in an hour?'
Thereat you smiled, and shook your golden head;
'Ah! not enough!' you said.
Then said I: 'Dear, it is not in my power
To tell how much, how many ways, my love;
Unnumbered are its ways even as all these,
Nor any depth so deep, nor height above,
May match therewith of any stars or seas.'
'I would hear more,' you smiled . . .

'Then, love,' I said,
'This will I do: unbind me all this gold
Too heavy for your head,
And, one by one, I'll count each shining thread,
And when the tale of all its wealth is told . . .'
'As much as that!' you said—
'Then the full sum of all my love I'll speak,
To the last unit tell the thing you ask . . .'
Thereat the gold, in gleaming torrents shed,
Fell loose adown each cheek,
Hiding you from me; I began my task.

''Twill last our lives,' you said.

Love's Exchange

Simple am I, I care no whit
For pelf or place,
It is enough for me to sit
And watch Dulcinea's face;
To mark the lights and shadows flit
Across the silver moon of it.

I have no other merchandise,
No stocks or shares,
No other gold but just what lies
In those deep eyes of hers;
And, sure, if all the world were wise,
It too would bank within her eyes.

I buy up all her smiles all day
With all my love,
And sell them back, cost-price, or, say,
A kiss or two above;
It is a speculation fine,
The profit must be always mine.

The world has many things, 'tis true,
To fill its time,
Far more important things to do
Than making love and rhyme;
Yet, if it asked me to advise,
I'd say—buy up Dulcinea's eyes!

Man the Destroyer

O spirit of Life, by whatsoe'er a name
Known among men, even as our fathers bent
Before thee, and as little children came
For counsel in Life's dread predicament,
Even we, with all our lore,
That only beckons, saddens and betrays,
Have no such key to the mysterious door
As he that kneels and prays.

The stern ascension of our climbing thought,
The martyred pilgrims of the soaring soul,
Bring us no nearer to the thing we sought,
But only tempt us further from the goal;
Yea! the eternal plan
Darkens with knowledge, and our weary skill
But makes us more of beast and less of man,
Fevered to hate and kill.

Loves flees with frightened eyes the world it knew,
Fades and dissolves and vanishes away,
And the sole art the sons of men pursue
Is to out-speed the slayer and to slay:
And lovely secrets won
From radiant nature and her magic laws
Serve but to stretch black deserts in the sun,
And glut destruction's jaws.

Life! is it sweet no more? the same blue sky
Arches the woods; the green earth, filled with trees,
Glories with song, happy it knows not why,

Painted with flowers, and warm with murmurous bees;
This earth, this golden home,
Where men, like unto gods, were wont to dwell,
Was all this builded, with the stars for dome,
For man to make it hell?

Was it for this life blossomed with fair arts,
That for some paltry leagues of stolen land,
Or some poor squabble of contending marts,
Murder shall smudge out with its reeking hand
Man's faith and fanes alike;
And man be man no more—but a brute brain,
A primal horror mailed and fanged to strike,
And bring the Dark again?

Fool of the Ages! fitfully wise in vain;
Surely the heavens shall laugh!—the long long climb
Up to the stars, to dash him down again!
And all the travail of slow-moving Time
And birth of radiant wings,
A dream of pain, an agony for naught!
Highest and lowest of created things,
Man, the proud fool of thought.

On the Morals of Poets

One says he is immoral, and points out
Warm sin in ruddy specks upon his soul:
Bigot, one folly of the man you flout
Is more to God than thy lean life is whole.

Orbits

Two stars once on their lonely way
Met in the heavenly height,
And they dreamed a dream they might shine alway
With undivided light;
Melt into one with a breathless throe,
And beam as one in the night.

And each forgot in the dream so strange
How desolately far
Swept on each path, for who shall change
The orbit of a star?

Yea, all was a dream, and they still must go
As lonely as they are.

Reliquiae

This is all that is left—this letter and this rose!
And do you, poor dreaming things, for a moment suppose
That your little fire shall burn for ever and ever on,
And this great fire be, all but these ashes, gone?

Flower! of course she is—but is she the only flower?
She must vanish like all the rest at the funeral hour,
And you that love her with brag of your all-conquering thew,
What, in the eyes of the gods, tall though you be, are you?

You and she are no more—yea! a little less than we;
And what is left of our loving is little enough to see;
Sweet the relics thereof—a rose, a letter, a glove—
That in the end is all that remains of the mightiest love.

Six-foot two! what of that? for Death is taller than he;
And, every moment, Death gathers flowers as fair as she;
And nothing you two can do, or plan or purpose or dream,
But will go the way of the wind and go the way of the stream.

Resurrection

Is it your face I see, your voice I hear?
Your face, your voice, again after these years!
O is your cheek once more against my cheek?
And is this blessed rain, angel, your tears?

You have come back,-how strange-out of the grave;
Its dreams are in your eyes, and still there clings
Dust of the grave on your vainglorious hair;
And a mysterious rust is on these rings-

The ring we gave each other, that young night
When the moon rose on our betrothal kiss;
When the sun rose upon our wedding day,
How wonderful it was to give you this!

I dreamed you were a bird or a wild flower,
Some changed lovely thing that was not you;

Maybe, I said, she is the morning star,
A radiance unfathomably far-

And now again you are so strangely near!
Your face, your voice, again after these years!
Is it your face I see, your voice I hear,
And is this blessed rain, angel, your tears?

Noon

Noon like a naked sword lies on the grass,
Heavy with gold, and Time itself doth drowse;
The little stream, too indolent to pass,
Loiters below the cloudy willow boughs,
That build amid the glare a shadowy house,
And with a Paradisal freshness brims
Amid cool-rooted reeds with glossy blade;
The antic water-fly above it skims,
And cows stand shadow-like in the green shade,
Or knee-deep in the grassy glimmer wade.

The earth in golden slumber dreaming lies,
Idly abloom, and nothing sings or moves,
Nor bird, nor bee; and even the butterflies,
Languid with noon, forget their painted loves,
Nor hath the woodland any talk of doves.
Only at times a little breeze will stir,
And send a ripple o'er the sleeping stream,
Or run its fingers through the willows' hair,
And sway the rushes momently agleam—
Then all fall back again into a dream.

The City In Moonlight

Dear city in the moonlight dreaming,
How changed and lovely is your face;
Where is the sordid busy scheming
That filled all day the market-place?

Was it but fancy that a rabble
Of money-changers bought and sold,
Filling with sacrilegious babble
This temple-court of solemn gold?

Ah no, poor captive-slave of Croesus,
His bond-maid all the toiling day,
You, like some hunted child of Jesus,
Steal out beneath the moon to pray.

The Last Tryst

The cowbells wander through the woods,
'Neath arching boughs a stream slips by,
In all the ferny solitude
A chipmunk and a butterfly
Are all that is—and you and I.

This summer day, with all its flowers,
With all its green and gold and blue,
Just for a little while is ours,
Just for a little—I and you:
Till the stars rise and bring the dew.

One perfect day to us is given;
Tomorrow—all the aching years;
This is our last short day in heaven,
The last of all our kisses nears—
Then life too arid even for tears.

Here, as the day ends, we two end,
Two that were one, we said, for ever;
We had Eternity to spend,
And laughed for joy to know that never
Two so divinely one could sever.

A year ago—how rich we seemed!
Like piles of gold our kisses lay,
Enough to last our lives we dreamed,
And lives to come, we used to say—
Yet are we at the last to-day.

The last, I say, yet scarce believe
What all my heart is black with knowing;
Doomed, I yet watch for some reprieve,
But know too well that love is going,
As sure as yonder stream is flowing.

Look round us how the hot sun burns
In plots of glory here and there,
Pouring its gold among the ferns:

So burned my lips upon your hair,
So rained our kisses, love, last year.

We saw not where a shadow loomed,
That, from its first auroral hour,
Our happy paradise fore-doomed;
A Fate within whose icy power
Love blooms as helpless as a flower.

Its shadow by the dial stands,
The golden moments shudder past,
Soon shall he smite apart our hands,
In vain we hold each other fast,
And the last kiss must come at last.

The last! then be it charged with fire,
With sacred passion wild and white,
With such a glory of desire,
We two shall vanish in its light,
And find each other in God's sight.

The Long Purposes of God

To Man in haste, flushed with impatient dreams
Of some great thing to do, so slowly done,
The long delay of Time all idle seems,
Idle the lordly leisure of the sun;
So splendid his design, so brief his span,
For all the faith with which his heart is burning,
He marvels, as he builds each shining plan,
That heaven's wheel should be so long in turning,
And God more slow in righteousness than Man.

Evil on evil mock him all about,
And all the forces of embattled wrong,
There are so many devils to cast out—
Save God be with him, how shall Man be strong?
With his own heart at war, to weakness prone,
And all the honeyed ways of joyous sinning,
How in this welter shall he hold his own,
And, single-handed, e'er have hopes of winning?
How shall he fight God's battle all alone?

He hath no lightnings in his puny hand,
Nor starry servitors to work his will,
Only his soul and his strong purpose planned,

His dream of goodness and his hate of ill;
He, but a handful of the eddying dust,
At the wind's fancy shaped, from nowhere blowing;
A moment man—then, with another gust,
A formless vapour into nowhere going,
Even as he dreams back into darkness thrust.

O so at least it seems—if life were his
A little longer! grant him thrice his years,
And God should see a better world than this,
Pure for the foul, and laughter for the tears:
So fierce a flame to burn the dross away
Dreams in his spark of life so swiftly fleeing:
If Man can do so much in one short day,
O strange it seems that an Eternal Being
Should in his purposes so long delay.

Easy to answer—lo! the unfathomed time
Gone ere each small perfection came to flower,
Ere soul shone dimly in the wastes of slime;
Wouldst thou turn Hell to Heaven in an hour?
Easy to say—God's purposes are long,
His ways and wonders far beyond our knowing,
He hath mysterious ministers even in wrong,
Sure is His harvest, though so long His sowing:
So say old poets with persuasive tongue.

And yet—and yet—it seems some swifter doom
From so august a hand might surely fall,
And all earth's rubbish in one flash consume,
And make an end of evil once for all . . .
But vain the questions and the answers vain,
Who knows but Man's impatience is God's doing?
Who knows if evil be so swiftly slain?
Be sure none shall escape, with God pursuing.
Question no more—but to your work again!

When The Long Day Has Faded

When the long day has faded to its end,
The flowers gone, and all the singing done,
And there is no companion left save Death-
Ah! there is one,
Though in her grave she lies this many a year,
Will send a violet made of her blue eyes,
A flowering whisper of her April breath,

Up through the sleeping grass to comfort me,
And in the April rain her tears shall fall.

We Are With France

We are with France—not by the ties
Of treaties made with tongue in cheek,
The ancient diplomatic lies,
The paper promises that seek
To hide the long maturing guile,
Planning destruction with a smile.

We are with France by bonds no seal
Of the stamped wax and tape can make,
Bonds no surprise of ambushed steel
With sneering devil's laughter break;
Nor need we any plighted speech
For our deep concord, each with each.

As ancient comrades tried and true
No new exchange of vows demand,
Each knows of old what each will do,
Nor needs to talk to understand;
So France with us and we with France—
Enough the gesture and the glance.

In a shared dream our loves began,
Together fought one fight and won,
The Dream Republican of Man,
And now as then our dream is one;
Still as of old our hearts unite
To dream and battle for the Right.

Nor memories alone are ours,
But purpose for the Future strong,
Across the seas two signal towers,
Keeping stern watch against the Wrong;
Seeking, with hearts of deep accord,
A better wisdom than the Sword.

We are with France, in brotherhood
Not of the spirit's task alone,
But kin in laughter of the blood:
Where Paris glitters in the sun,
A second home, like boys, we find,
And leave our grown-up cares behind.

Sunset in the City

Above the town a monstrous wheel is turning,
With glowing spokes of red,
Low in the west its fiery axle burning;
And, lost amid the spaces overhead,
A vague white moth, the moon, is fluttering.

Above the town an azure sea is flowing,
'Mid long peninsulas of shining sand,
From opal unto pearl the moon is growing,
Dropped like a shell upon the changing strand.

Within the town the streets grow strange and haunted,
And, dark against the western lakes of green,
The buildings change to temples, and unwonted
Shadows and sounds creep in where day has been.

Within the town, the lamps of sin are flaring,
Poor foolish men that know not what ye are!
Tired traffic still upon his feet is faring-
Two lovers meet and kiss and watch a star.

What of the Darkness?

What of the darkness? Is it very fair?
Are there great calms and find ye silence there?
Like soft-shut lilies all your faces glow
With some strange peace our faces never know,
With some great faith our faces never dare.
Dwells it in Darkness? Do you find it there?

Is it a Bosom where tired heads may lie?
Is it a Mouth to kiss our weeping dry?
Is it a Hand to still the pulse's leap?
Is it a Voice that holds the runes of sleep?
Day shows us not such comfort anywhere.
Dwells it in Darkness? Do you find it there?

Out of the Day's deceiving light we call,
Day that shows man so great and God so small,
That hides the stars and magnifies the grass;
O is the Darkness too a lying glass,

Or, undistracted, do you find truth there?
What of the Darkness? Is it very fair?

Richard Le Gallienne – A Concise Bibliography

My Ladies' Sonnets and Other Vain and Amatorious Verses (1887)
Volumes in Folio (1889) poems
George Meredith: Some Characteristics (1890)
The Book-Bills of Narcissus (1891)
English Poems (1892)
The Religion of a Literary Man (1893)
Robert Louis Stevenson: An Elegy and Other Poems (1895)
Quest of the Golden Girl (1896) novel
Prose Fancies (1896)
Retrospective Reviews (1896)
Rubaiyat of Omar Khayyam (1897)
If I Were God (1897)
The Romance of Zion Chapel (1898)
In Praise of Bishop Valentine (1898)
Young Lives (1899)
Sleeping Beauty and Other Prose Fancies (1900)
The Worshipper of The Image (1900)
The Love Letters of the King, or The Life Romantic (1901)
An Old Country House (1902)
Odes from the Divan of Hafiz (1903) translation
Old Love Stories Retold (1904)
Painted Shadows (1904)
Romances of Old France (1905)
Little Dinners with the Sphinx and other Prose Fancies (1907)
Omar Repentant (1908)
Wagner's Tristan and Isolde (1909) Translator
Attitudes and Avowals (1910) essays
October Vagabonds (1910)
New Poems (1910)
The Maker of Rainbows and Other Fairy-Tales and Fables (1912)
The Lonely Dancer and Other Poems (1913)
The Highway to Happiness (1913)
Vanishing Roads and Other Essays (1915)
The Silk-Hat Soldier and Other Poems in War Time (1915)
The Chain Invisible (1916)
Pieces of Eight (1918)
The Junk-Man and Other Poems (1920)
A Jongleur Strayed (1922) poems
Woodstock: An Essay (1923)
The Romantic '90s (1925) memoirs
The Romance of Perfume (1928)

There Was a Ship (1930)
From a Paris Garret (1936) memoirs
The Diary of Samuel Pepys (editor)

www.ingramcontent.com/pod-product-compliance
Lightning Source LLC
Chambersburg PA
CBHW060104050426
42448CB00011B/2614